WORKING AS IF LIFE MATTERED

Best wishes
Margaret Lulic

Working As If Life Mattered

All rights reserved.
Copyright © 1995 by Margaret A. Lulic

No part of this book may be reproduced in any form or by any means, electronic or mechanical, including information storage and retrieval systems, without written permission from the publisher, except by a reviewer who may quote brief passages in a review.

Published by
Blue Edge Publishing
5057 Upton Avenue South
Minneapolis, Minnesota 55410

ISBN 0-9638526-1-2

Here For A Purpose

HERE FOR A PURPOSE

I think of mission (for a company or individual) as concrete and specific. It's what we make or do. That can change...Purpose is different. It doesn't change, and in a sense, is on a higher playing field or a deeper one. It's what you can't not do or can't not be.
                                    Wynne Miller

HERE FOR A PURPOSE

Work is the way you express your personal purpose in the world.   Linda Marks

You really are the moment of truth.   Jan Calzon

HERE FOR A PURPOSE

As managers our fundamental purpose is to build a department and organization that we are proud of. Our unit in many ways becomes a living monument to our deepest beliefs in what is possible at work...Each time we act as a living example of how we want the organization to operate, it is a positive political act.

Peter Block

HERE FOR A PURPOSE

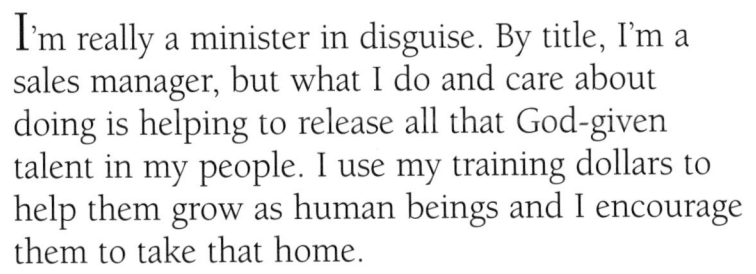

I'm really a minister in disguise. By title, I'm a sales manager, but what I do and care about doing is helping to release all that God-given talent in my people. I use my training dollars to help them grow as human beings and I encourage them to take that home.

Sales director

HERE FOR A PURPOSE

Hold fast to dreams
For if dreams die
Life is a broken winged bird
That cannot fly.

Langston Hughes

HERE FOR A PURPOSE

A Person is not a thing or a process but an opening through which the Absolute can manifest. Heidegger

I shall never believe that God plays dice with the world. Albert Einstein

HERE FOR A PURPOSE

There must be a sense that what I do is somehow congruent with the overall purpose, design, and flow of the universe as I experience it. I've got to feel that my work fits with the big picture.

Larry Dossey

HERE FOR A PURPOSE

Man's main task in life is to give birth to himself.
                                        Erich Fromm

Our own life is the instrument with which we experiment with truth.

                                        Thich Nhat Hanh

HERE FOR A PURPOSE

The Buddha, in his wisdom, made "right livelihood"...one of the steps to enlightenment. If we do not pitch our discussion that high, we have failed to give work its true dimension, and we will settle for far too little —perhaps for no more than a living wage.

Theodore Roszak

HERE FOR A PURPOSE

I believe God calls each and every human being to civility. This means we are all under the obligation to become more conscious, to grow in spiritual competence, and to strive to be ethical in our behavior...In making the choice to accept this...one's life becomes very different—much more constructive, more rich, more fulfilling.

M. Scott Peck

HERE FOR A PURPOSE

We have all the questions every other company has. In addition, we ask, "What is the company here for in the biggest sense? What are we in this for?" What really matters around here is to live with questions about the meaning of life.

Steve Wikstrom

HERE FOR A PURPOSE

We are not human beings having a spiritual experience. We are spiritual beings having a human experience.   Teilhard De Chardin

I have come to see that the greatest mark is made not by what we do but through who we are.
         Linda Marks

HERE FOR A PURPOSE

When we try to pick out anything by itself, we find it hitched to everything else in the universe.
                                             John Muir

There is greatness buried in each soul from the moment of birth. It shows up in our need to matter, to know we make a difference.
                                             Margaret Lulic

HERE FOR A PURPOSE

I'm in the printing industry. I've got a job I enjoy, working with people I like. I have a nice home and wonderful family. I have it made. So why do I feel this longing for something else? I had this crazy dream. It was about Gandhi and me and something about peacemaking. I don't get it but it was powerful. Do other people have dreams like this? I'll never know because I'd be afraid to ask.

Printer

HERE FOR A PURPOSE

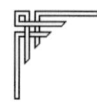

Children truly are our greatest gift as well as our greatest teachers. They ask that we be loving, calm, caring, attentive, trusting, playful, honest, and mature. ...It has been said that adults do not create children but rather that children create adults. Robert Roskind

HERE FOR A PURPOSE

We are all moved by compassion, inspired by truth, touched by care, heartened by hope, stirred by love, and emboldened by courage. This is the commonality of being, the irreducible is.

Thomas Thiss

HERE FOR A PURPOSE

A random Universe assumes the planet is a result of a huge hit or miss evolution. Belief in a punitive God assumes the planet is a testing field, or race course. ...Some will win, many will lose....(A) third model, however, assumes that the planet is a huge schoolroom, from which every student will eventually graduate. The curriculum has only one lesson to teach and that is unconditional love in all circumstances.
— Robert Roskind

Longings

LONGINGS

I have discovered I am not alone in wondering about living a more meaningful life. I have had many informational interviews...in new product development, business development, and marketing...in industrial and consumer markets. Ninety percent (of those people) have been going through some kind of crisis within their jobs...People are re-examining their lives and asking what they really want.
                                             Susan James

LONGINGS

That is happiness: to be dissolved into something complete and great.   Willa Cather

It is not death that a man should fear, but he should fear never beginning to live.
                    Marcus Aurelius

LONGINGS

I am continually amazed at the number of people...who tell me they would love to be doing something else if it were not for financial commitments and other obligations...I suspect that we could free ourselves from more of this than we care to admit...we are trapped by "golden handcuffs" and are far less in charge of our future than we would like to be.   Dan Hanson

LONGINGS

You have got to own your days and name them, each of them, every one of them, or else the years go right by and none of them belong to you.
            Herb Gardner

(Compared to two decades ago) the average employed person is now on the job an additional 163 hours, or the equivalent of an extra month a year.   Juliet Schor

LONGINGS

My mother was physically failing, though mentally alert as ever. I couldn't take care of her any more and basically forced her to agree to go to a nursing home. I know how much that hurt her and I see it taking a toll on her. If I only had 5-10 more hours a week it would make all the difference. An adult worker/parent/caregiver

LONGINGS

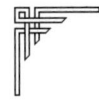

Most people have work that is too small for their spirits.

Studs Terkel

LONGINGS

I spend my life rushing. I rush the kids through breakfast, dash to day care, speed to work, go from one thing to another at work, eat a quick lunch at my desk, keep going all afternoon. Then I run home to fix dinner before going off to some evening commitment. I wish I could slow down.

         A working mom

LONGINGS

Hurt people hurt people.
Healed people heal people.

In and through community lies the salvation
of the world.   M. Scott Peck

LONGINGS

I'm close to retirement. All my life I've played by the rules. Now, society wants to change them. They want to change retirement benefits because they say we are robbing the young. I get angry when I hear this or read it in the paper. And I protest loudly. In the still of the night, though, I think about my grandkids and I know there is some truth in what they say. What kind of system do we have that pits the young against the old?

Senior citizen

LONGINGS

What's it going to take for white people to see my humanness? What do I tell my children to expect in life? I see racial and ethnic tensions increasing and I'm not sure what we do about that.   A sales representative

LONGINGS

I've been down-sized and right-sized and re-engineered and now I'm under-employed.
I wonder if there will ever be another real job.
I have two college age kids. I don't know how we're going to do it.

                    A "50-something" plant engineer

LONGINGS

I wish my company did good in the world. There is a difference between not doing harm and actually doing good. I think it could help me find that extra inspiration and energy to keep going when I'm exhausted and bored. It would be nice to go home and answer my daughter's questions about what I do with more meaning and pride.

A factory worker

LONGINGS

From a biblical perspective, the word for spirit is Ruah, meaning breath. When we lose our Ruah, we lose our spirit, we no longer have inspiration, even though our external world doesn't see it....We can still perform our jobs well throughout this experience. And then there is the hook. I don't care what we do for a living, there is something about a job that hooks us... So we feel caught between these feelings.

Richelle Pearl Koller

LONGINGS

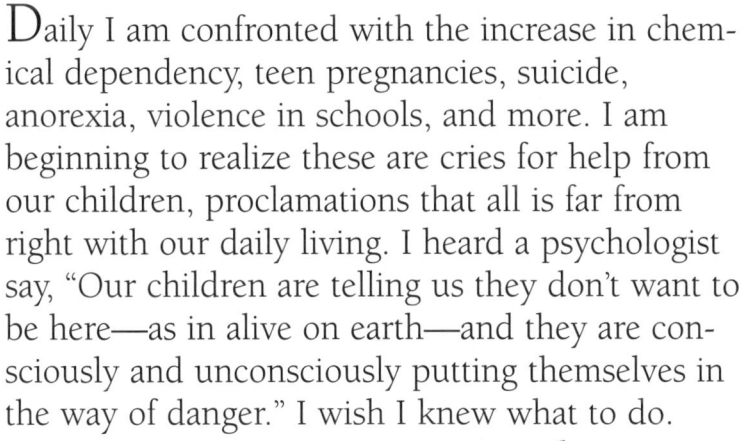

Daily I am confronted with the increase in chemical dependency, teen pregnancies, suicide, anorexia, violence in schools, and more. I am beginning to realize these are cries for help from our children, proclamations that all is far from right with our daily living. I heard a psychologist say, "Our children are telling us they don't want to be here—as in alive on earth—and they are consciously and unconsciously putting themselves in the way of danger." I wish I knew what to do.

A teacher

LONGINGS

I want...to live "in grace" as much of the time as possible....I mean an inner harmony; essentially spiritual, which can be translated into outer harmony. In this first happy condition (graced), one seems to carry all one's tasks before one lightly, as if borne along on a great tide; and in the opposite state (out of grace) one can hardly tie a shoestring.

                                    Anne Morrow Lindbergh

The System Isn't Working

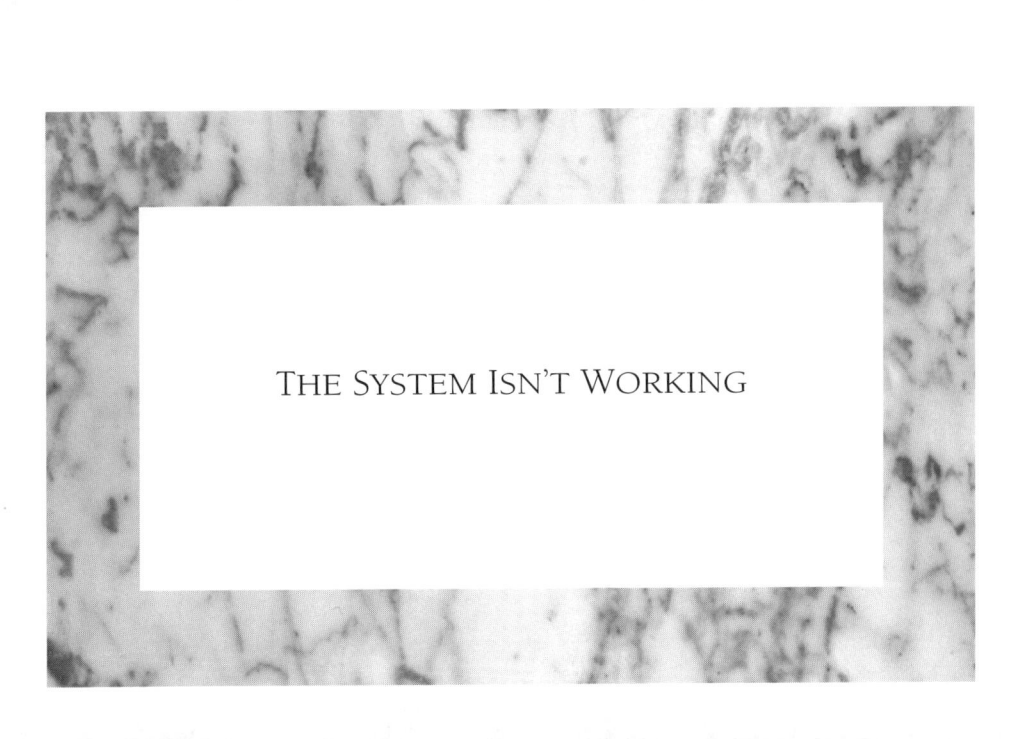

THE SYSTEM ISN'T WORKING

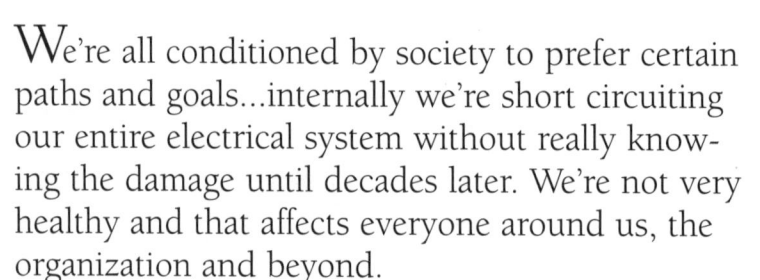

We're all conditioned by society to prefer certain paths and goals...internally we're short circuiting our entire electrical system without really knowing the damage until decades later. We're not very healthy and that affects everyone around us, the organization and beyond.

Chuck Denny

THE SYSTEM ISN'T WORKING

We worked unlimited hours, as plant managers, to cover all the bases in the old system. We were doing it for the money, and really, at a cost to our families since we were gone so much. As a result some of us had ulcers and other problems. When our goal is not correct, it's going to stress our spiritual sides, too.

Robert Suelflow

THE SYSTEM ISN'T WORKING

The first few times we circled the earth, we saw the United States, Europe, Asia, Africa and the Soviet Union. But as we moved further into space, those imaginary lines began to disappear and we saw that we were one. This profoundly affected many of us. Amidst all the beauty was the profound realization that all was not right with the earth. —Edgar Mitchell

THE SYSTEM ISN'T WORKING

If the world were a town of 1000 people there would be 564 Asians, 210 Europeans, 86 Africans, 80 South Americans, and 60 North Americans. 700 people would be illiterate and 500 would be hungry.
                    Ligget-Stashower Public Relations firm

Following that distribution, about 250 people would be consuming 70% of the energy, 75% of all metals, and 85% of the wood.   Margaret Lulic

THE SYSTEM ISN'T WORKING

It seems absurd for business to invest so much money and time in the education of our young people and then have such backward policies and norms that affect parents in the workplace. It's like we are shooting ourselves in the foot.

Margaret Lulic

THE SYSTEM ISN'T WORKING

For most companies, the result of downsizing and layoffs is that they are then inadequately staffed to do a decent job. Companies are expecting sixty, seventy, eighty hour work weeks, especially from managers. People can't work at those levels for long periods of time without burning out... without having very serious health problems, even death. ...There are thousands of people out there who are dying inside.   Robert Carlson

THE SYSTEM ISN'T WORKING

We tend to meet any new situation by reorganizing. And a wonderful method it can be for creating the illusion of progress while producing inefficiency and demoralization.
                        Petronius   A.D. 65

THE SYSTEM ISN'T WORKING

Life without meaning is the torture
Of restlessness and vague desire -
It is a boat longing for the sea and yet afraid.
                Elgar Lee Masters

THE SYSTEM ISN'T WORKING

Too much emphasis on money reverses the whole picture; you then become the servant, and the money becomes the master. Earl Nightingale

Our life is frittered away by detail...Simplify, simplify.   Thoreau

THE SYSTEM ISN'T WORKING

It is not the life of simplicity but the life of multiplicity that the wise men warn us of...It does not bring grace; if destroys the soul...It is not merely the concern of the American as such, but of our whole modern civilization, since life in America today is upheld as the ideal for a large part of the rest of the world...perhaps a first step, is in simplification of life, in cutting out some of the distractions.   Anne Morrow Lindbergh

THE SYSTEM ISN'T WORKING

Sleep has been another casualty of modern life. According to sleep researchers, studies point to a "sleep deficit" among Americans, a majority of whom are currently getting between 60 and 90 minutes less a night than they should for optimum health and performance.   Juliet Schor

THE SYSTEM ISN'T WORKING

Economist Victor Fuchs has found that between 1960 and 1986 the time parents actually had available to be with children fell ten hours a week for whites and twelve for blacks. Hewlett links the parenting deficit to a variety of problems plaguing the country's youth: poor performance in school, mental problems, drug and alcohol use, and teen suicide.   Juliet Schor

THE SYSTEM ISN'T WORKING

One of the great ironies of our present situation is that overwork for the majority has been accompanied by the growth of enforced idleness for the minority. Just as surely as our economic system is "under producing" leisure for some, it is "overproducing" it for others. (This includes underemployment as well as unemployment)
            Juliet Schor

THE SYSTEM ISN'T WORKING

...Realize that if we took the total number of hours the typical adult spends watching television during the course of the entire year, it adds up to...the equivalent of two entire months. We do this even though we say we don't really like much of the programming.

The Barna Report

THE SYSTEM ISN'T WORKING

Within the span of a few centuries the focus of interest shifted from the inner world to the outer world...All but one of the (seven deadly) sins, sloth, was transformed into a virtue. Greed, avarice, envy, gluttony, luxury, and pride were the driving forces of the new economy.

                                        Lewis Mumford

THE SYSTEM ISN'T WORKING

We are alienated from nature...We are alienated from our work, since that has in so many cases become devoid of meaning. We are alienated from each other...And, being deeply confused about our own being, we are alienated from ourselves.
          Willis Harman and John Hormann

THE SYSTEM ISN'T WORKING

Every American consumes about 36 pounds of resources a week, while 2000 pounds of waste are discarded to support that consumption.

If one year's supply of a cleaner for a community is 10,000 bottles, the total purchase price of $30,000 is slotted this way:
$9,300 for packaging, $4,200 in various taxes,
$6,900 for labor, $800 in actual raw material,
$3,400 in overhead and marketing,
$5,400 to insurance companies, truckers,
and sundry taxes.

Paul Hawken

THE SYSTEM ISN'T WORKING

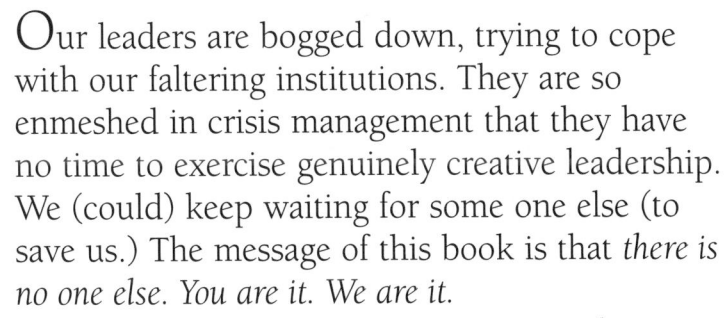

Our leaders are bogged down, trying to cope with our faltering institutions. They are so enmeshed in crisis management that they have no time to exercise genuinely creative leadership. We (could) keep waiting for some one else (to save us.) The message of this book is that *there is no one else. You are it. We are it.*

Duane Elgin

Real Possibilities

REAL POSSIBILITIES

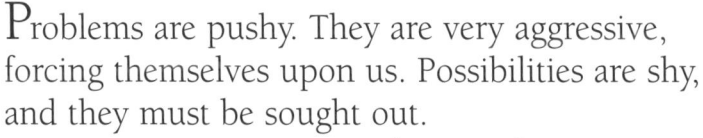

Problems are pushy. They are very aggressive, forcing themselves upon us. Possibilities are shy, and they must be sought out.

          Thomas Thiss

REAL POSSIBILITIES

One of the transformations that could take place is reducing the work week...This could help resolve the current ludicrous situation where some people are working sixty to one hundred hours a week...while others are not working at all... This...would give us more time for our families, for doing more things for ourselves, for volunteering or working on community projects.
       Corrine McLaughlin & Gordon Davidson

REAL POSSIBILITIES

Growing numbers of well-established, high-achieving women...are insisting on a new work ethic, one that does not require them to spend... their lives working sixty- and seventy-hour weeks, leaving no room in their lives for anything but the career chase. Susan Albert

REAL POSSIBILITIES

Perhaps we're being pushed —individually and collectively—into a higher level of functioning. It would be a nice part of our mythos, I should think, if this chaos so many of us feel really weren't a problem but an opening: a door onto a new relationship to time, where only half our task is getting life to do what we want it to do. The other half is discovering where life itself wants us to go.   Marjorie Kelly

REAL POSSIBILITIES

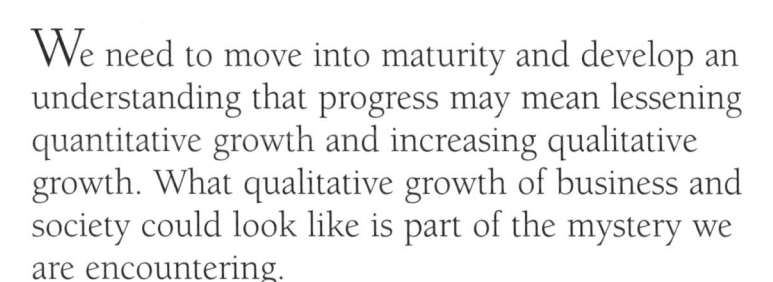

We need to move into maturity and develop an understanding that progress may mean lessening quantitative growth and increasing qualitative growth. What qualitative growth of business and society could look like is part of the mystery we are encountering.

Barbara Shipka

REAL POSSIBILITIES

(A quiet movement toward voluntary simplicity is under way.) It involves a deliberate organization of life for a purpose...a manner of living that is outwardly more simple and inwardly more rich;...a deliberate choice to live with less in the belief that more of life will be returned to us in the process.   Duane Elgin

REAL POSSIBILITIES

We need to explore new alternatives that allow everyone to make a contribution and, in return, receive a way to live decently. Creating a system based on meaningful contribution may mean that our current ways of employment totally disappear because they represent an insufficient idea. "Contribution" is a much larger framework.
Barbara Shipka

REAL POSSIBILITIES

Experiments are under way around the country with a new form of "money." Combining elements of barter, volunteer time, debit card technology, and corporate discounts, people can contribute to their community and receive buying power in return. This is a new twist on doing what you love and receiving something tangible in return. Even more important, it brings new options for participating in the economy to those who have been left out of it.

Margaret Lulic

REAL POSSIBILITIES

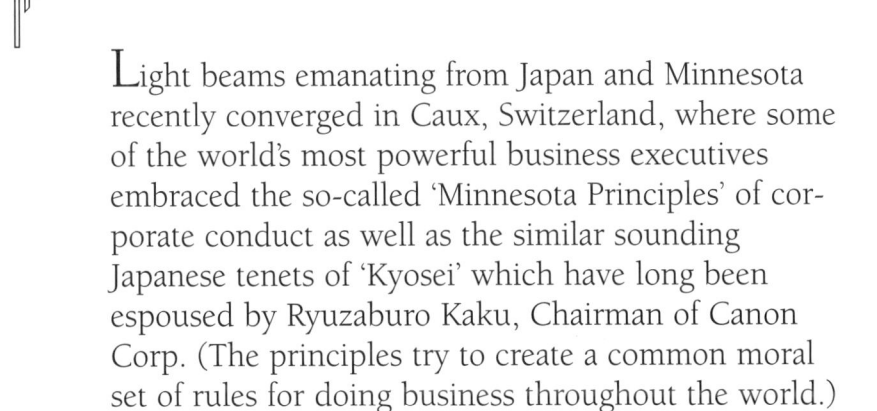

Light beams emanating from Japan and Minnesota recently converged in Caux, Switzerland, where some of the world's most powerful business executives embraced the so-called 'Minnesota Principles' of corporate conduct as well as the similar sounding Japanese tenets of 'Kyosei' which have long been espoused by Ryuzaburo Kaku, Chairman of Canon Corp. (The principles try to create a common moral set of rules for doing business throughout the world.)

John Oslund

REAL POSSIBILITIES

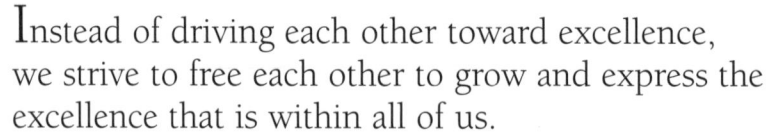

Instead of driving each other toward excellence, we strive to free each other to grow and express the excellence that is within all of us.
                                   Steve Wikstrom

While eating is critical to living, one does not live to eat. So profits were critical to (the company's) health, but they weren't the bottom line.
                                   Steve Wikstrom

REAL POSSIBILITIES

What if marketing developed so that the customer was sensitized into experiencing higher order needs? ...(Then) the business of business would be to raise the consciousness of the market.
Jagdish Parikh

REAL POSSIBILITIES

A Third Wave of the environmental movement is upon us, led by some of the most unlikely activists you can imagine: corporate executives. And it's not regulations that are driving them, it's their own values. Something profoundly new is at work here: a social movement, beginning not at the fringes of power, but at its very center.

Sally Power and Craig Cox

REAL POSSIBILITIES

(A possible principle for sustainable small business) would be to replace national and internationally produced items with products created locally and regionally...communities export less capital while depleting fewer resources.

Paul Hawken

REAL POSSIBILITIES

Nature is...cyclical; there is virtually no waste in the natural world that does not provide food for other living systems. We need to create an economy that duplicates nature's cycle where the waste from one process is the food for another.

Paul Hawken

REAL POSSIBILITIES

If I am living my purpose and vision, I will live from a place of inspiration. If I am inspired, others will...find their own fire, passion and reason for doing things well. When we find that, it is bigger than we are; it is beyond us and we will feel a genuine desire to do what is right. I want my employees to give what they have because they love what we are doing. Terri Lynn

REAL POSSIBILITIES

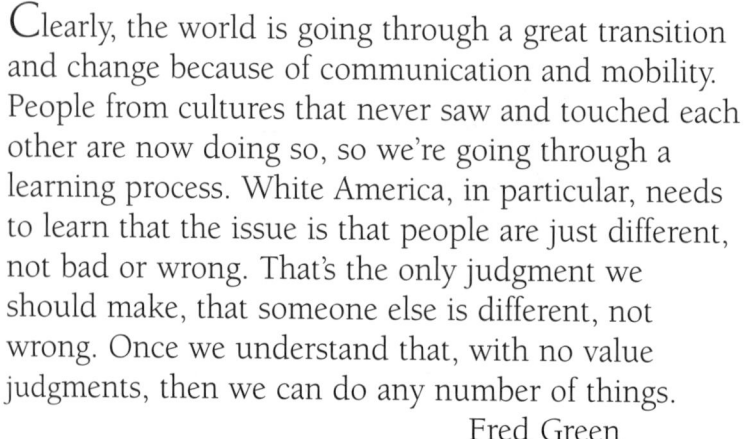

Clearly, the world is going through a great transition and change because of communication and mobility. People from cultures that never saw and touched each other are now doing so, so we're going through a learning process. White America, in particular, needs to learn that the issue is that people are just different, not bad or wrong. That's the only judgment we should make, that someone else is different, not wrong. Once we understand that, with no value judgments, then we can do any number of things.

Fred Green

REAL POSSIBILITIES

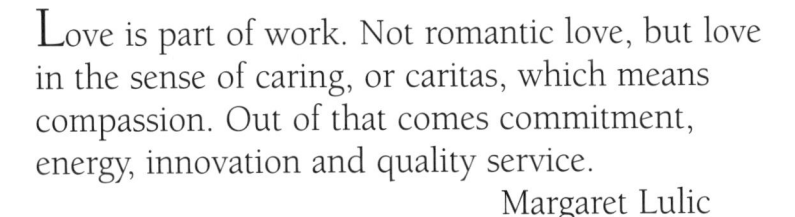

Love is part of work. Not romantic love, but love in the sense of caring, or caritas, which means compassion. Out of that comes commitment, energy, innovation and quality service.

Margaret Lulic

REAL POSSIBILITIES

I've learned the questions are sometimes more challenging than getting to answers. I've learned doubt is part of growth...There are ditches on both sides of any road. The challenge is to live with questions, not to always come up with the answer. Steve Wikstrom

REAL POSSIBILITIES

I believe a good boss must be able to relate to people's spiritual needs—if not directly, then by recognizing that our individual desire to touch heaven, to seek that spark of divinity within each of us, is the greatest power on earth. It is the force that motivates all people, and must be so recognized to unleash the tremendous force for good that resides in each and everyone of us.

George McCown

REAL POSSIBILITIES

...Many of the people I come in contact with are seeing their work or business as their teacher—the bottom line, if you will, for applying what they've learned in their spiritual practices—perhaps the most demanding "guru" of all. Work has become the new spiritual classroom.

David Gershon

REAL POSSIBILITIES

If only we had the wisdom and patience to... explore the work in which we are now engaged, to explore ourselves, we'll usually find the riches we seek, whether they be financial or intangible or both.   Earl Nightingale

REAL POSSIBILITIES

What if owners and employees were the same persons? This is true in the Spanish Association of Mondragon Cooperatives. Every employee must loan the cooperative about $10,000. When a new person starts work, he or she signs a note and over time the amount is withheld from their salary without any interest changes. Thus, everyone is invested in their own business.

Margaret Lulic

REAL POSSIBILITIES

I'm less fearful now when I hear a rumor (about another company change coming) because I know I'll adapt to whatever the situation is. I'm learning I can handle anything that comes along...I feel like a flower that has been allowed to blossom.
Sandy Miller

REAL POSSIBILITIES

There is never a training session in which I am not greatly moved by the courage of people to change incredibly difficult things in their work, family, and spiritual life...I know that the human spirit is indomitable...if the spark is still ignited, if we haven't gone to sleep or sold out spiritually, people are much alike and can do incredible things.
                                                Gail Straub

REAL POSSIBILITIES

I think we all have had experiences where someone may not have even known they were changing our lives. Looking back, we recognize turning points that may have seemed insignificant at the time...So we have to have faith and believe in what we cannot see.

Fred Green

REAL POSSIBILITIES

I believe deeply that no prayer is ever unanswered. I have no doubt about that. They aren't always answered the way we would like to see them answered, but in some way that is a mystery to all of us, they are answered.

Guy Schoenecker

REAL POSSIBILITIES

Let the word go forth from this time and place, that the torch has been passed to a new generation of Americans...So let us begin anew...The energy, the faith, the devotion which we bring to this endeavor will light our country and all who serve—and the glow from that fire can truly light the world.

John Kennedy

REAL POSSIBILITIES

When we undertake change efforts...we can know we have the potential of significant effects on our communities. Our companies can become prisms of positive change. Our employees can become the prisms that change our world.

Margaret Lulic

REAL POSSIBILITIES

Never doubt that a small group of thoughtful, committed citizens can change the world. Indeed it is the only thing that ever has. Margaret Mead

Studies have found an idea becomes a dominant way of thinking when 20% of the population adopts the idea...
   Corinne McLaughlin and Gordon Davidson

REAL POSSIBILITIES

The salvation of this human world lies nowhere else than in the human heart, in the human power to reflect, in human meekness and in human responsibility. Without a global revolution in the sphere of human consciousness, nothing will change for the better in the sphere of our being as humans, and the catastrophe toward which this world is headed—be it ecological, social, demographic, or a general breakdown of civilization—will be inevitable.

    Vaclav Havel, President of Czechoslovakia

REAL POSSIBILITIES

When historians look back on the 20th century they will say that the most significant change was the change of the mind, a quiet, but pervasive change of the mind.

Willis Harman

REAL POSSIBILITIES

We're reaching the point where the change process becomes much faster....It may have taken us ten years to get to that point, but from there on, it isn't ten more years to get the same distance. It's more like in one year, we've changed more than we did in ten and the next year we're changing the same degree in three months.

Fred Green

REAL POSSIBILITIES

My personal opinion is that any further improvement of the world will occur by having individuals make quality decisions and that's all. God, I don't want any more big programs full of social planning for big masses of people that leave individual quality out.

Robert Pirsig

REAL POSSIBILITIES

During the conference the Maharishi suggested that if only 1 percent of a population began to meditate and experienced consciousness, the remaining 99 percent of the population would also be affected. The idea was certainly unorthodox, but it could be tested, and sociologist Garland Landrift did just that....He found that for the 1% cities (without meditation groups) the crime rates...*increased* an average of 8.3%. But in each of the non-1% cities (with meditation groups) there was a *decrease* in the crime rate of 8.2%. The likelihood that these findings could have occurred by chance was less than one in a thousand.

Larry Dossey

CREATING THE CHANGE WE SEEK

CREATING THE CHANGE WE SEEK

Much of life is a paradox. We find that that which is personal drives the business, that what is known as the right (receptive) brain drives the left (active) brain, the metaphorical drives logic, and that which may seem non-productive drives productivity. Basically, we have discovered that the intangibles drive the tangibles.

Magaly Rodriguez

CREATING THE CHANGE WE SEEK

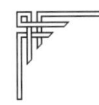

Creativity is not being able to use every color in the spectrum. It's about having only two and making miracles with them. Art is discovered by restrictions. Use restrictions as an impulse to creativity.

Magaly Rodriguez

CREATING THE CHANGE WE SEEK

There is no Answer, but there are answers: love and the joy of working, and the simple pleasures of food and fresh clothes, the little things that tend to get lost and trampled in the search for the Grand Solution to the Problem of Life and emerge, like the proverbial bluebird of happiness, only when we have stopped searching.

Harold Kushner

CREATING THE CHANGE WE SEEK

If we can see clearly what's really important in our deepest core and be willing to be humbled in order to try to achieve it, we can breakthrough. And should it appear that we failed, we need to know we haven't failed, but that some good will come sooner or later.

Margaret Lulic

CREATING THE CHANGE WE SEEK

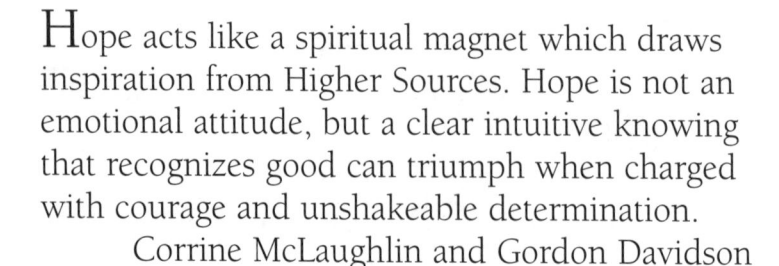

Hope acts like a spiritual magnet which draws inspiration from Higher Sources. Hope is not an emotional attitude, but a clear intuitive knowing that recognizes good can triumph when charged with courage and unshakeable determination.
      Corrine McLaughlin and Gordon Davidson

CREATING THE CHANGE WE SEEK

The modern hero, the modern individual who dares to heed the call and see the mansion of that presence with whom it is our whole destiny to be atoned, cannot, indeed must not, wait for his community...It is not society that is to guide and save the creative hero, but precisely the reverse.
Joseph Campbell

CREATING THE CHANGE WE SEEK

...The moment one definitely commits oneself, then Providence moves, too. All sorts of things occur to help one that would never otherwise have occurred...all manner of unforeseen incidents and meetings and material assistance, which no man could have dreamed would have come his way.   Goethe

CREATING THE CHANGE WE SEEK

Thinking will not overcome fear, but action will.
            W. Clement Stone

As soon as a person makes up his or her mind to take the plunge into adventure, they are aware of a new strength they did not think they had, which rescues them from all their perplexities.
            Dr. Paul Tournier

CREATING THE CHANGE WE SEEK

We must learn to step forward without the grand plan and without overcoming all possible objections.   Margaret Lulic

Much of life passes by as we sit and worry. Estimates are that 40% of what we worry about never happens and 30% is about what is done and unchangeable.   Margaret Lulic

CREATING THE CHANGE WE SEEK

The best way to predict the future is to create it.
Peter Drucker

If it is to be, it is up to me.

Unknown

CREATING THE CHANGE WE SEEK

Every moment of your life you are offered the opportunity to choose love or fear, to tread the earth or soar to the heavens.

                                                  Emmanuel

Few things will liberate you faster and move you more quickly along your inner path than doing the things you fear.

                                         Elaine St. James

CREATING THE CHANGE WE SEEK

It costs so much to be a full human being that there are very few who have the enlightenment, or the courage, to pay the price...One has to abandon altogether the search for security, and reach out to the risk of living with both arms.

Morris L. West

CREATING THE CHANGE WE SEEK

I have expanded my boundaries farther than I ever imagined. So maybe they aren't really there. They may be self-imposed limitations.

                                                          Jeff Zibley

CREATING THE CHANGE WE SEEK

The trick is, to be willing to walk through, even though we don't know what is on the other side (of the unknown.). Maybe it's like swimming; we have to believe the water will hold us...
>Richelle Pearl Koller

CREATING THE CHANGE WE SEEK

Most of what we call pain is actually our experience of resistance to the phenomena... And the resistance is usually a good deal more painful than the original sensation.

Stephen Levine

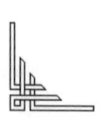

CREATING THE CHANGE WE SEEK

Two of the most painful things a person can experience physically are the passing of kidney stones and giving birth. From a physical perspective, these two events are nearly identical in pain and intensity. But we experience them very differently because birth is meaningful and kidney stones are not.

Stephen Levine

CREATING THE CHANGE WE SEEK

Be patient with all that is unresolved in your heart
And try to love the questions themselves
Do not seek for the answers that cannot be given
For you would not be able to live them
And the point is to live everything
Live the questions now
And perhaps without knowing it
You will live along some day
Into the answers

> Ranier Maria Rilke

CREATING THE CHANGE WE SEEK

We are born with sparks for many virtues. Which ones we choose to ignite and to what degree we ignite them affects the quality of our lives and of all those around us. It is on this bedrock that we can build a new life.

Margaret Lulic

CREATNG THE CHANGE WE SEEK

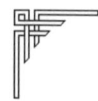

Scientists have proven that it's impossible to long jump 30 feet, but I don't listen to that kind of talk. Thoughts like that have a way of sinking down to your feet.

      Carl Lewis, Olympic athlete.

CREATING THE CHANGE WE SEEK

Medical research demonstrates that prayers work. People who prayed for strangers who didn't know they were being prayed for were statistically more likely to heal better. If prayer works that has to mean something about the nature of the universe. We need to each decide what the meaning is for us.

Larry Dossey

CREATING THE CHANGE WE SEEK

When we don't voluntarily take up the big questions, life hits us with an emotional punch. Today's organizational downsizing is creating the external stimulus for many people to ask new and old questions. The maturing of the baby boomers is another stimulus. We're beginning a new phase of life with global implications.

Margaret Lulic

CREATING THE CHANGE WE SEEK

We must look *at* the lens through which we see the world, as well as *at* the world we see, and that the lens itself shapes how we interpret the world.
Stephen Covey

Lessons From Geese: Geese fly in formation with a common direction and sense of community. This formation adds 71% greater flying range than if a bird flew alone.
Milton Olson

Inner Explorations

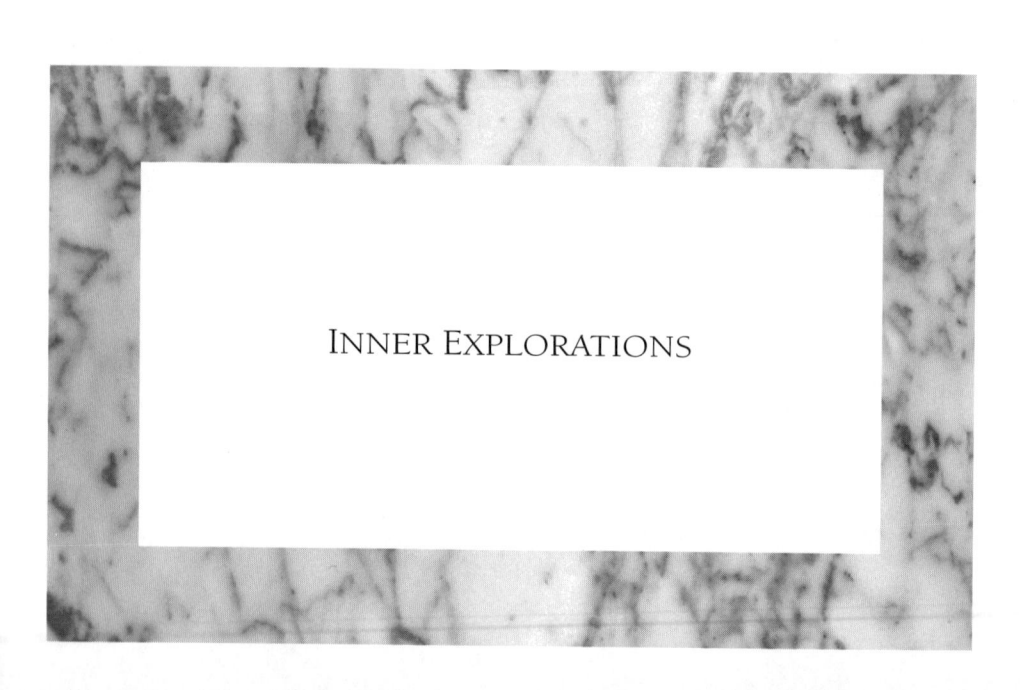

INNER EXPLORATIONS

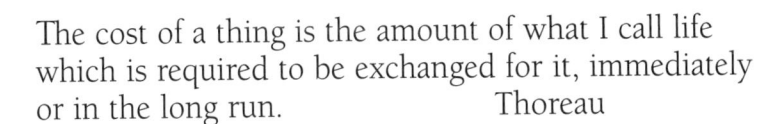

The cost of a thing is the amount of what I call life which is required to be exchanged for it, immediately or in the long run.   Thoreau

We are all painfully aware of the distractions, clutter, and pretense that weigh upon our lives and make our passage through the world more cumbersome and awkward. To live with simplicity is to unburden our lives.   Duane Elgin

How much of my life have I exchanged for my material possessions? How do I feel about the quality of this exchange? How might I unburden my life?

INNER EXPLORATIONS

We have to ask what message we are sending to our children, spouses, family members, and friends when we spend fifty, sixty, or seventy hours a week in our work lives and only a few hours a week with them. No matter how much we may feel we love them, it sends the message that we value them far less than our careers and herein lies the damage we do.

Robert Roskind

What message might my work week be sending to those I care for? What questions do I want to ask?

INNER EXPLORATIONS

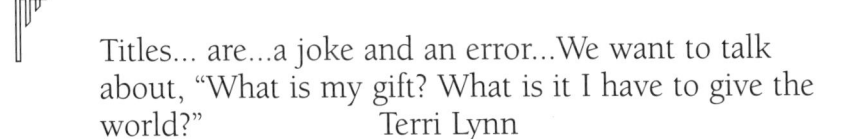

Titles... are...a joke and an error...We want to talk about, "What is my gift? What is it I have to give the world?"   Terri Lynn

I am of the opinion that my life belongs to the whole community and...it is my privilege to do for it whatever I can... Life is no "brief candle" to me. It is a sort of splendid torch that I have got hold of for the moment, and I want to make burn as brightly as possible before handing it on to other generations.
George Bernard Shaw

Can I see that I too carry a torch, a gift, that could burn more brightly?

INNER EXPLORATIONS

Let us build the earth by building one another.
Pierre Teilhard De Chardin

I wonder how many times I have stilled a song.
Daniel Hanson

When have I built another and when have I stilled someone else's song?

INNER EXPLORATIONS

It's easier to spend your life manipulating an institution than it is dealing with your own soul. It truly is. We make institutions sound complicated and hard and rigorous, but they are a piece of cake compared with our inner workings.   Parker Palmer

We must be the change we wish to see in the world.
                                                                    Gandhi

What change do I need to embody to create the organization or world I desire?

INNER EXPLORATIONS

A calling is when a deep gladness in your heart meets a deep need in the world.   Frederick Buechner

I don't know what your destiny will be, but one thing I do know; the ones among you who will be really happy are those who have sought and found how to serve.
                                       Albert Schweitzer

What is my calling?

INNER EXPLORATIONS

The highest reward for man's toil is not what he gets for it, but what he becomes by it.   John Ruskin

It is good to have an end to journey toward; but it is the journey that matters, in the end.

Ursula K. Le Guin

What am I becoming through my current toil? Do I desire something else?

INNER EXPLORATIONS

If there is this universal energy field that we're all plugged into, then we would see ourselves as a sort of transmitter and receiver in this field. The more clear we are about our purpose, the better we transmit. The more we become an open receiver, the more we have all those important experiences that appear coincidental.

Wynne Miller

For one day let me pretend there are miracles.

INNER EXPLORATIONS

The real voyage of discovery lies not in finding new landscapes, but in having new eyes.
                              Marcel Proust

The opportunity: To make the most ordinary moments extraordinary.   Unknown

How can I take one ordinary routine and infuse it with new life?

INNER EXPLORATIONS

We are all the architects of the future. When you have an inspiration, take note. It may only come through once.   Jacqueline Small

The formation of hypotheses is the most mysterious (experience)...A person is sitting somewhere minding his own business and suddenly-flash-he understands something he didn't understand before.
     Robert Pirsig

How do I treat my flashes, my inspiration?

INNER EXPLORATIONS

The greatest despair is to not become the person you were meant to be.   Kierkegaard

We believe that there is a learner in all of us who may be asleep, as a result of education and life experiences. When people awaken that learner within, they become hungry for growth and change.
Magaly Rodriguez

Am I awake or sleep walking through life? Am I growing into who I was meant to be?

INNER EXPLORATIONS

Nature moves 50,000 gallons of water suspended in mid air all around the earth with no organization chart or strategic plan.   Margaret Wheatley

The heroes of all time have gone before us...and where we had thought to find an abomination, we shall find a god; where we had thought to travel outward, we shall come to the center of our own existence; where we had thought to be alone, we shall be with all the world.   Joseph Campbell

How has nature equipped me to be a hero or heroine?

INNER EXPLORATIONS

Do we work to live or live to work?

                                                        Max Weber

Whatever you can do, or dream you can, begin it. Boldness has genius, power and magic in it. Begin it now.   Goethe

What dream could I begin?

Margaret A. Lulic, M.A., is a consultant, coach, and speaker on personal and organizational change. She graduated from Marquette University and the University of Chicago. Add twenty plus years of work experience in diverse areas of business, adjunct faculty experience at the University of St. Thomas, and parenting. Her first book, *Who We Could Be at Work,* demonstrated she is a master at fusing the practical, the intellectual, the spiritual and the emotional at work. It offers a vision of what work could be through the stories of real people and companies.

Available from bookstores and by phone from:
Image Group International
1-800-708-0558